Why Not Me

I dedicate this book to my sister for her motivation, the inspiration I received from my nephews and my mother for making sure the project was completed.

Why Not Me

"A Common Sense Approach to Self-Awareness and Team Building"

Brenda Winston

AuthorHouse™
1663 Liberty Drive
Bloomington, IN 47403
www.authorhouse.com
Phone: 1-800-839-8640

First published by AuthorHouse   07/14/2011

ISBN: 978-1-4634-1502-0 (sc)
ISBN: 978-1-4634-1501-3 (ebk)

Library of Congress Control Number: 2011909152

Printed in the United States of America

Any people depicted in stock imagery provided by Thinkstock are models, and such images are being used for illustrative purposes only.
Certain stock imagery © Thinkstock.

This book is printed on acid-free paper.

I. Who Am I
   1) What makes me smile
   2) What do I believe
   3) What motivates me
   4) What is my passion

II. How do People See me
   1) Do I make people happy
   2) Am I simply heard or do people listen
   3) Is my advise sort after
   4) Is my advise used

III. How do I see myself
   1) Am I happy
   2) Am I satisfied with being heard or do I need people to listen
   3) Am I a mentor, if so, do I enjoy it
   4) Do I follow up

IV. Dream, Plan, Execute and Achieve
   1) Are my dreams small or big, black & white or in color
   2) What is my motivational level
   3) What is the time frame from dream to plan
   4) Is the goal attainable

V. The Good Life
   1) How does one live well
   2) What is the cost
   3) Does the ends justify the means
   4) Did the journey make you smile

I

Who am I

"Try not to become a man of success but rather to become a man of value."
Albert Einstein (1879 -1955)

As you begin to figure out who you are, it's good to start with the simple things. A lot of what we do is attributed to who we are. A lot of what we say is due to how we see ourselves, and how we think others see us. Let's start with the simplest of all…

1) What makes me smile

To smile is a wonderful thing. It allows for amusement, pleasure and affection. When something gives you that happy feeling it is hard to bet against it. Every chance you get you ought to smile, and the more you smile the more amusement and pleasure you bring to your life and others.

To smile is one thing; but, to understand what makes us smile is another. We recognize the power of a smile, so what makes us smile? We know what it brings to our lives so how can we capture it? How can we recreate the situation that brought us that amusement? I guess if we knew the answer, we could solve many problems. So let's narrow it down the best way we can, and view this from the rear view mirror of our lives.

The object is to simplify the process. We don't want to analyze a lot of situations prior to taking action, but we must review our steps and see where we go from here. A smile is the first step towards achieving the best in ourselves. When we smile we look fondly on things…remembering the good times.

It's so important that we do those things that make us smile, those things that causes us to reflect on the good times. When R & B Singer Al Green sang *"For the Good Times"* it was at a time when many

Americans were shut out of the American Dream yet they found something to smile about; something that brought them pleasure and amusement. They reflected on those good times, and smiled. As hard as it was for them, they held on to the good times, so what's stopping us?

As we reflect on the troubled history of America; we may wonder what caused so many of them, who were left out of the American Dream to smile. Well whatever it was, they found it, they captured it and they used it. With every opportunity, they duplicated that vision and smiled every chance they could: embracing the Good Times. Our task is not to duplicate what they did; we can't. Their memories are different from ours. What we must do is, use that gift of a smile to praise ourselves for what's going right and motivate us to create new value while remaining optimistic.

For many of us it's not just one thing. That's good. This allows us to pull on several things to garner the same feeling. We are a multi-facetted people, we have different emotions and those emotions are driven by different occurrences. So it's never just one thing that makes us smile, rather a series of things. Our job is to pinpoint what causes us to smile and do that thing or things as often as possible. The ability to smile is something we can never lose.

If a group of people can smile in their most desperate times, if they can move forward with that happy feeling then why can't we.

First, let's put in perspective what happens when we smile...many times when we smile we are happy. And that happiness comes from within. When we are happy we are content and we are filled with pleasure and satisfaction. No one can doubt the power of being happy, being content and being satisfied. So now our question is what can get us there? The first step is to smile.

The happy feeling that makes us smile comes from within. But what outside force can we capture to bring about the same event. For each of us it is different so we must identify it and keep it close.

There are times we wake up to a bright sunny day and smile, knowing that today will be better than yesterday. As for me, when I lecture to a group: I say simply, *"I got out of bed today because I believe today will be better than yesterday."* Now my question is; do I truly believe that? If so, do I ascribe to that belief?

If I hold those simple truths, then I can easily muster up a smile. I can live with simple things knowing what makes me smile is within my grasp. A smile is not just something that we can put on for a picture. It is not something we can request on command. A smile is brought on through something we feel deep inside, something we can share. This smile is a powerful thing.

After my lectures, the group leaves the session feeling empowered knowing they have gathered the information needed to be better. They leave the session believing their role is just as important as anyone else's and they have the power to change their lives. Simply by choosing what is right for them, they elevate themselves to a higher level of understanding. So the question is: what allows us to do this? And how do we recognize it?

This will be different for each of us. I remember taking a trip in high school and seeing a new place for the first time. It was a good time. I flew out of my hometown with my High School Classmates and Friends. It was my first trip to Washington, DC; our nation's capital. I traveled knowing how important the trip would be; especially since I was and still am a history buff. I knew I had to take in and enjoy each moment. I was in awe of the various memorial buildings – from The White House to the Washington Monument. I was intrigued with the Lincoln Memorial and the Kennedy Center for the Arts, mainly because I understood the roles those presidents played in shaping the history of our country. I also viewed the Cherry Blossom Parade understanding it celebrates Japan's gift of trees to the United States in 1912. And would never forget how I felt strolling down The National Mall, where Dr. King gave his famous *"I have a Dream Speech"*.

I also visited the other side of our nation's capital, the side simply known as DC, and was stunned. Shaken by what I saw, I recognized the separation of the haves from the have not. As a young person it was hard to conceptualize. One thing for sure, I left Washington, DC in April 1982 – changed. I now had a clearer view of US History and an understanding of how different worlds can co-exist. I witnessed each community's sense of pride, their measure of happiness and their ability to smile.

I would reflect on that trip many times after and at each time it would make me smile. That was my first time seeing things as they are; and within minutes, see the same city as it ought to be. That trip would play a huge role in my life. It would allow me to see splendor and misery in the same day. It would allow me to see beyond the picture, beyond the outward appearance and treasure the hopeful feeling of it all.

Most of all the memory would bring me back to the person who made it happen – my mother. She was the one who made sure I gained that memory. She was the force behind my trip; and she had no way of knowing it would become the benchmark for many things in my life. So today, as I reflect on that trip; I smile and it continues to bring me joy.

So as we revisit the times of our lives we wonder what makes us smile. It does not matter what it is, all that matters is that we smile. As we shape ourselves and configure our lives we must identify what makes us smile.

Look within you, re-connect with that moment, or create new ones. Go back to that place that delivered on a promise for you, a place that allowed you to grow and develop. Find out what it is, connect those dots, recreate those moments and smile. We are all at our best when we smile.

2) What do I believe

As we go about our daily lives we do those things that matter to us. We do those things that add benefit, and allow us to grow. Through this journey we become more aware of our surroundings, more aware of our ties and connections to each other. Many of us have a solid belief structure rooted in our family history and values.

Still there are those among us who pull together our belief structure as we matriculate through life. One thing for certain, it is important for us to shape some sort of belief structure.

It is in our belief we gain our strength and move forward. With that in mind we must identify it. So how do we do that?

Many of us design our belief on what has been passed down to us. Some of us call it God; others say a Supreme Being and still others look to a center force.

The key to this belief structure is-knowing the role it plays in our development. Even after we use all the tools in our arsenal the yearning for something to believe in continues. What we believe may provide that extra courage needed to go on. What we believe allows us to shape our position as we face challenges. When we exhibit our inner grace under pressure, it stems from what we believe.

With that in mind, it is imperative we recognize what it is we believe, and call on it every time as we shape our views.

I grew up a good Catholic Girl, kneeling at the altar of our church, confessing my sins to our Priest; yet wondering was I forgiven. I remember uttering the prayers I was given, but not feeling any different at the end. I was going through the motions, not questioning why or how, but doing what was expected. I was doing my due diligence…so to speak.

Even then, I just followed the code. I did not know what to expect so I just did what I was told. One thing for sure, I relied on people to give me directives; because, I trusted them. Truly I believed in them. I also knew they would not stir me wrong. They were my family they were my support unit; they were my rock.

Though I did not know what the connection would be, or the true meaning of what I was doing; I knew I had to do it because it was expected. As an adult, I began to put into perspective my own belief structure. The belief that will allow me to seize the moment: and insure my advancement. I remember going through life simply acting correctly in the presence of those who would stand in judgment of me. Doing everything by the book; *smooth sailing* must have been my mantra. I played it safe. That safety net helped me through my childhood; but would it be useful as an adult.

Following *"The Golden Rule"* without question ~ is the path of least resistance. Additionally, I had a keen understanding of picking my battles. I never attempted to challenge the power structure. But is that the way to be all you can be? Simply allowing a problem to exist, while believing it will work itself out was my method…but was it right?

As we are all called to do things greater than ourselves…Is just following the *"Golden Rule"* the best approach? Now in reflection; I must ask myself, were my behavior as a child the right one? Would it be of benefit to me as an adult?

In any regard, I had to come to terms with what I needed for further development. So as I crafted my course and moved toward higher ground and bigger things, I had to identify my personal belief.

Personal character always pushes you towards those things that are bigger than yourself. Just doing things that affect only you will not be a driving force. When I decided to join my sorority ~ it was based on what they did and how they carried themselves on the college campus.

Growing up with a value system based on Christian principles played a huge role in my development –

both my grandmother and mother advised me on the art of *"being seen and not heard"*. So between my family's Catholic Faith and my structured home life, I operated like a well-oiled machine. Everyone in our family knew their role and stayed in their lane. My two sisters' and I did what was expected and what we were told. We did well in school, followed the rules of the day and stayed out of trouble. To be honest, we had no other options. We could not opt out of the plan.

No one had to check our homework and our mother was never called into school for an impromptu parent-teacher conference. We simple did what we were told. Basically that was all we knew, and it worked well for our family. We never challenged authority.

This rule driven, Catholic proven household would shape my belief structure and character as a child; but what role would it play in my adult life?

Looking back, I don't believe I missed out on much. Even though I did not challenge, nor questioned authority, my childhood was good. I had fun and I learned how to enjoy the journey. The questions I have today are: while I did what was expected did I get to do what I wanted? How would this inability to challenge authority shape me now?

Thankfully, I became a good citizen. I studied, earned a college degree, became a Teacher, and enjoyed it.

My childhood was the path of least resistance. It taught me to walk away rather than face a challenge. But in retrospect, it left me vulnerable in certain areas; not comfortable in facing issues head on.

As an adult, when I was pushed, I would retreat. As I experienced hardships; I would not demonstrate my worth or value, nor would I fight for what I wanted. I did not understand that real success required fighting for your belief. Nor did I realize the need to take risks, and most of all – to let go of fear.

This brings me to the pomp and circumstance of our church, the foundation of my belief system. Its great strength lies with its doctrine or *"rites of passage"*. These programs further aligned me to the practicality of life. I learned those rites well and move through my Catholic Sacraments as I grew. I never jumped in front of the line; I earned each step. I never lost those fundamental principles of working hard toward being better and moving at an attainable pace while making sure I did the basic things that allowed me to succeed.

Those proceedings gave me more structure and principle; but where would they fit in my belief system? Those things are real, and they are solid; but would they be enough? I had to dig deeper to find my substance and my sense of purpose. Not having all the answers can be burdensome, and nagging. But taking time to figure it out; made me vulnerable. When I found myself not knowing what to do next, I felt scared.

Then I realized: to be all I can, and do all I can; I must identify what I believe. When you believe you can do something you will break down barriers. When you realize you can do what you want, you feel whole. You identify with it.

As an adult, my goal has always been the greater good. I believe the desire to do more, and be more, is right. For me, a yearning to serve; ranks very high. But how would I achieve that?

So then I went back to the structure and principles I learned growing up and aligned them with my work. While doing that, I realized facing down challenges builds character. And with character you become fearless. And fearlessness is needed for success.

Knowing that is one thing, doing it, is another. How do you manifest something you never learned or even tried? How do you get pass the critics who challenge you while you're on the road to succeed?

Each one of us must move pass those issues in our own way. For me it came full circle. To achieve success, I had to find my inner force that would allow me to take risks and become fearless. I had to seize the fearless power, and call on it daily. Then I recognized my belief couldn't be based on external factors rather it must be internal. My belief system must be tied to a greater power. The power that has brought me to this day: the natural power of Love.

The power of Love allows me to connect with others; it forces me to see myself in others. I believe once we look at each other and see a little bit of ourselves; we won't hurt each other. It's not just the word love; rather, the feeling of love. Although my structured and principled upbringing helped ground me, love in its true sense, built me.

As I frame my view, I understand the power of love and its connection to a higher power. I recognize my views are based on love and stem from love. The things that have built me up and played a role in my development are not foreign to love. In fact, love is at their core. As I look out and see the big picture, I know love is the bridge.

As a college student I embraced everything around me and took everything in. I surrounded myself with people who cared about me and who loved me. Again I was in a safe place, a comfort zone. Now it's time to take those feelings on the road. To chart a course that would allow me to blossom.

When I am in an unwelcoming environment, when I am tested and surrounded by people who may not wish me well, what do I do? How do I battle for me…my future and my legacy…knowing the real world allows for friend and foe to co-exist.

To be successful one must be able to confront and engage. Yet I was taught not to confront, not to challenge. I learned the best way was to remain busy and contribute at the highest level without seeking attention. Embedded in me was the art of staying above the fray, without attachments. So I grew without concern for single mastery and without defending a cause; this behavior could only go so far.

I grew without battling to the end. Without challenging information where appropriate. I lost hold of the successful module, which created fear and doubt. With the idea of staying above the fray, I lost that attention to the detail needed for positive impact.

It was then I realized I had to begin to challenge. I had to seek out the details which allowed for better understanding and communication. It also allowed for compromise and bridge building.

With my belief structure in tack, I began to see things more creatively and recognize their value.

In cultivating my belief, I remember talking with one of my nephews, at the time he was 7or 8. I asked him about his goals; at which time he boldly looked me in the eye and said he will go to college, because it was in his genes. He knew then that failure was not an option; he was fearless.

You see as a child his success was rooted in love. He saw his life as a big game, on a big stage; and he was the Quarterback. He studied his game plan but was not afraid to call an audible as different challenges approached him.

So when I think of him and his desire to succeed, I am pushed to do more, using his words as inspiration: *"because it is in my genes"*.

I would use the power of love to bridge gaps in my life, to face challenges and build my future plans. So when asked, what do I believe…my answer has to be: whatever I do must be based on *Love*.

3) What motivates me

Everyone knows about the carrot and the stick; one motivates and the other puts you back in line. What drives you to do all you can? And how do you get enough to keep you going each day? Now you know the importance of finding out what you believe in and the need to fight for it...How do you do it? You need a motivator! This motivator will be your trigger to keep you going.

You need this motivator to wake you up, to point you in the right direction and to find the light in the darkness. Once you can pinpoint your carrot or *motivator*, you will stay on message; you will stay in the game and the arena will remain open to you.

This arena is your playing field; where various people are together. Some of those people may be your family and friends; some may be your adversaries and some you may not even know. But what should be clear to you is the role each one of them must play as you move toward your success. You need each one to participate like a team, for you to ultimately succeed.

This motivator calls you to action; it gives you that desire to do something. Though we are what we are, at the same time, we are always becoming. Though we sit in a particular position; many times, we want more or something different. So as we move through life we have to constantly challenge ourselves to seek more, do more and be more. That is the part of us that understands there is still much work to do. It is that part of us that says never give up and pushes us further. How do we uncover that part of us?

Begin with surrounding ourselves with our family and friends; they allow us to quickly broaden our tent. So it is important for us to commune with those people and stay in fellowship with them.

In your bleakest hour, they can help re-affirm and renew you. Your need for their presence is important, they keep your grounded.

The power of family and friends is common in many successful stories; many people refer to them as *"The wind beneath their wings"*. Because they love you, they will wish you well. They know where you have been, understand where you are and believe in where you are going. It is those ties that truly bind, allowing you to stay the course.

If that is all that surrounds you, then life would be a *"bed of roses"*, but it's not. Our lives are filled with peaks and valleys, highs and lows, lemons and lemonade. The good thing is our motivator will help us find more peaks, more highs and drink more lemonade than the alternatives. Your motivator can help you understand the difference between securing a job or doing your life's work.

Surrounding yourself with the people who wish you well is positive and could be empowering. When doubt comes in the picture, it's good to have someone say you can keep going…your goal is at hand.

I remember in college and right after, I was filled with confidence. When I believed I could do anything, but in a blink of an eye it all came crashing down. Reality rushed in and said welcome to the big leagues. As I grew older I realized everyone in the arena brought their "A" game, and everyone wanted to win.

As I matriculated down the field, I encountered more competitors than family and friends. I was exposed to things that I had never seen, and at times was not prepared for. For a long time I would look at the field, play the game then retreated to my world of security and comfort. I continued this pattern over and over again, until I realized I was not getting the success my family and friends believed I could achieve. Most importantly the result I got was not what I wanted.

When I realized I wanted a different result, I had to take a different approach. I could not continue with the status quo hoping to get a winning result. After all I was not insane. I had to try something different to make a difference.

This new approach enabled me to disarm my adversaries and make my life what I wanted. This was my euphoric moment; it was at that time I knew I was on my way. I began to identify various areas of my life and started to connect the dots. I activated what worked, released what did not and built a new foundation.

I had to learn that everyone else couldn't be wrong every time; I played a role in my shortcomings as well. The key to gaining what I wanted required me to be at peace and to secure serenity. To attain that comfort zone, I had to see a part of me in everyone who played on my team. I had to learn how to stand out without sticking out. I had to show patience in an urgent environment to build on my success.

So I looked around the field, saw my family, friends and competitors; but then that was only one third of the arena. I was then moved at the possibilities of bringing the other two-thirds along. Then I realized to do that successfully, I needed motivation.

Wikipedia explains motivation as the set of reasons that encourages one to engage in a particular behavior. According to various theories, motivation may be rooted in the basic need to minimize physical pain and maximize pleasure. No one wants to work hard every day of their life; they aspire to achieve a plateau where they can enjoy the fruits of their labor. That in itself is a motivational force. People must see what's in it for them, what they will gain by aligning with me.

To remain focused on my success, I had to seek my motivating force and unleash it as I moved toward the goal. I recognized my joy comes naturally and I can call upon it by reflecting on the good times of my life.

Achieving my goal will require more than just those things; it will take an assembly of minds working collectively for a cause. So I looked at this as an opportunity to introduce myself to the two-thirds of the arena that was strange to me. They didn't know my name or what I stood for…at least not yet.

What a great place to be in, a chance to introduce yourself, to shape your message and build your team. Right now I have the microphone, I am in control, and I know myself best.

So what will push me to speak on my behalf? It has to be the same thing that urges me to press on. My motivator must be at my core, and I must call on it daily. Few can wake-up and just do it, still others can glide into it, but many need that extra push, the strength to go on and persevere.

A few years back, when my nephew heard I would be joining them in St. Thomas on a family trip. He said, *"Aunty Brenda's coming…you know what that means…she's going to make a list and say check after completing each activity."* He was right. That is exactly what I do, and have been doing all my life. That approach speaks to my structural and principled upbringing. Some may view this as anal; I know one of my managers did. She told me how she got a kick out of reading my daily agenda, left on my desk for the next day.

One thing I know is, those lists allowed me to complete each tasks in a timely manner; with minimum physical force and maximum success.

As each task was checked off, I felt a degree of achievement. As I completed each one, I knew I could do the next one. Setting and reaching small goals kept me in the game. I was motivated daily by those achievements, no matter how small.

So it's clear, my motivator is achievement. I am driven by saying, *"job done"*. Once it's on my agenda or my list, I know I have to do it. I am motivated by each component that I see, knowing the great feeling that awaits me at completion.

Each of us must find what motivates us, because we will need it to face our challenges. We must lean on those who give us strength, disarm those who mean us harm and define ourselves to those who watch us. Our motivator is within, showing us ways to accept where we are…and believe where we can go.

4) What is my passion

To succeed you need passion. When you remain in the middle or neutral in a time of crisis, this approach does not convey confidence or success. The most successful people are very passionate about what they do. They have strong feelings for their passion and they are enthused by it. The successful ballplayer is passionate about his game. He does those things that will elevate it, those things that will align him or her with the great players of the day or immortalize him or her with the best to play the game.

As an avid sports fan; I wonder what the greatest players of the game were thinking as they came to work each day. Did they set out to be immortalized or were they just playing because of their love and skill for the game.

I enjoy watching a good player perform at his or her best. It amazes me to see them do those things the rest of us can only imagine. Setting records that no one could possibly catch, yet understanding when those records were matched and surpassed, that was the reason for setting the records in the first place.

The sporting arena is no different from the arena of life. We must report each day eager to start a new. We must be eager to build on our individual records so that the team could advance. Many ballplayers who have won their sport's MVP Award would gladly give it up for a championship ring. Many stay in the game longer just to experience that championship moment. They are passionate about winning. They live by the Lombardi Credo which says *"winning isn't everything, it is the only thing"*. That drive to win is infectious and pushes the team's agenda.

We must develop that type of spirit in our everyday life; that desire to win. After all, no one wants to lose or be around a loser and worst of all participate on a losing team. The team with the most wins usually has the best players. Outsiders look at them and want to be like them, they become the standard bearer. They are the models that others want to imitate. Everyone wants to know what got them to where they are. Their plays and plans are duplicated over and over again as the model of success.

Even though they set the standard for winning, they don't have the only pattern to success. There is no one way to win every time. If that were the case the same team would continue to win. There is no silver bullet for winning, but there is a passion that lives in the winner and that passion can be shared.

That passion pushes you to stand up even in the face of adversity, recognizing that challenges introduce you to yourself. The challenge forces you to consider what you should do to help this team win. When you are passionate, you will focus and participate in the activities of the arena. That same passion can produce a forward thinker with a soft power. This passion does not seek credit. It determines the tone you will take with your team and it will breed better communication.

So now the question is: are you doing what you are most passionate about, or are you on the bench of a losing team?

Your passion may require some risks, as you move towards your life's work. After all, your goal can not be to remain on the bench of a defeated team, getting paid every Monday, but loosing.

We are not always certain how everything will turn out, so why not try something new. You must determine what you want to win and go full speed ahead towards the winner's circle.

As for me, to find my passion; I have to embrace strong emotion and release the concept of over thinking. I have to fight for what I believe to be right. If I do that, my passion will grow and I will carve out a place for me. Knowing I am fighting for my own place on this winning team, I will be better equipped to take some degree of risk.

Now that I know what passion can accomplish; I know what I must do. I must be passionate enough about the goals I set, so I can stay the course. Even when I lose my way, I must learn from it and develop alternate ways to get to the goal.

My passion will help me find the means to reach the goal at the end. Many times the means have a cost and there are many risks. But if you remain on the right side of the issue then the cost will be justified. If your passion is for the greater good...the way to it will be right.

You must remember no one is perfect but as an achiever you must continue to better yourself by continuously adjusting your strategy so you can win. If you give yourself the time to reflect...so that nothing becomes tragic...nothing overwhelms you, then the goal will be yours.

Allowing yourself to change those things that you can while accepting those things you cannot change is the formula for winning. You will be comforted by the serenity of the journey and your passion will flow.

Chapter 1 Recap ~ WHO AM I

- Identify yourself first in simple terms; you must know who you are and what makes you smile.

- Identify what you believe in and what keeps you going.

- What you believe and what motivates you may be two different things. Understanding both and being able to interchange them when needed, will allow you to find your passion.

- Your passion will push you; it will keep you going.

II

How do People See me

"Success in business requires training and discipline and hard work. But if you're not frightened by these things, the opportunities are just as great today as they ever were."
David Rockefeller (1915 -)

1) Do I make people happy?

We can't judge our happiness by others; but we can gain fulfillment by making others happy. We shouldn't set out to make x number of people happy on any given day; but we can make a point to elevate individuals throughout the day.

As a leader with the plan to build a good team around you, it is important that your players are excited, motivated and believe they are a part of a good team. First you should assign everyone a role. People tend to rise to the position once they know their part. Your next step is to create a winning environment by defining the goal, so when the tide rises, all boats will be lifted.

A few years ago, one of my nephews asked me for a hand held electronic game. At the time, he was a good boy and he still is, so it was easy to reward him. Even though the game was very expensive and he also needed a pair of tennis shoes, I felt compelled to oblige. After all, how do you not reward a kid when he's doing good work.

I knew when he mentioned what he wanted, what I had to do. Also I wanted to surprise him. It was his birthday and it was important that he be happy on that day.

So it was a no brainier, I quickly bought both items the tennis shoes and the electronic game and wrapped them together. This allowed for an element of surprise.

The one thing I did not know was prior to his big day he spoke to his younger brother about it. That same brother tried to convince him that he would not get the game, since it was... *"so expensive."*

On his birthday, he came to my home and saw the gift wrapped in an oversized box. Right away, his brother shouted, *"I told you, I told you she wouldn't buy it."* It was at that moment I smiled and patiently watched him open the gift. He looked disappointed and a little discouraged for he knew he had done all he could to get what he really wanted. After all he was a good boy.

To his surprise the electronic game was wrapped in a smaller package with the tennis shoes. At that moment, I realized how it felt to make someone really happy. His shout, his smile, his share joy was priceless.

Former First Lady Barbara Bush said, *"Never lose sight of the fact that the most important yardstick of your success will be how you treat other people."* Making people happy, wishing them well, greeting them with a smile will be to your benefit. When you have true joy and happiness within, you can give it freely. This makes you feel good about yourself and good about others. Before you know it, others will recognize your goodness and be drawn towards you.

Our lives are not based on just making people happy, but there is great reward in sharing good news and making others comfortable in our presence. There is something to be said for disarming your advisories. Allowing them to be themselves and feel comfortable around you.

To make someone happy may require you to buy a gift, share a good word or flash a smile. The key when delivering those things is using the right tone.

On that note, there are people who speak in tones that leave other individuals out. They use English as a second language around regular folks. They use words their group may not understand, nor care to learn. This type of communication is pointless.

I know one such gentleman who speaks very fast and seems to be using every word in the thesaurus. His communication leaves much to be desired. Whenever he speaks, I get breathless. I wonder if he truly knows his audience. What exactly is his desire? Is he trying to uplift the people around him? Or is he simply trying to show off his knowledge of the English Language? Regardless of his mission, it can't be good. When regular folks feel they have to run to a dictionary after listening to you, they're not likely to follow you.

In that regard you will lose their heart and soul. Your groups' comfort level will be gone. Their desire to let their hair down in your presence will disappear.

So this can't be the path towards making someone happy. Even if you are giving that person good information; if your group does not understand what you are saying the feeling of joy or happiness won't blossom.

So to make someone happy, you must communicate your idea in such a way that the person grasps the information at delivery. The best way to receive happiness is to first give it. The concept of making someone happy must become a part of your daily life. Happiness can't be planned or regimented, happiness is selfless.

Good communication is needed and it can make someone happy. In sharing happiness: anger, jealously, ill will and resentment, are lifted away, and you will be better for it. This process of sharing good news is to your benefit. You feel better about yourself and others.

By making others happy, you will look with wonder at the great things that lay ahead. You will see others as they should be, strong and independent. By sharing goodwill, you grow wiser in joy and true happiness.

As an operations manager for many businesses, I recognized the importance of sharing a good word with the sales team. It is good for them to receive an optimistic remark to start their day. The sales team should be reminded of the great operations group behind them. This helps them face down and better deal with unflattering comments from the outside.

I've worked with many sales people and they encounter both highs and lows daily. Many times their emotions reflect their day. They are excited when they close a big deal and may become depressed when a sale is pending or rejected. It is at that time, the inside team must make them happy. You must uplift them. It helps them and it helps you.

So to the defining question, do I make people happy; that answer should be YES! If by chance you can't answer in the affirmative, then you have some work to do. The process of making others happy is a part of your journey to the goal.

Start by showing appreciation. Remember it is better to be kind than to always be right.

2) Am I simply heard or do people listen to me

Since we believe a good word can make someone happy, it can also make their day. That good word can serve as a springboard to many things. So we must make sure our words are not just heard but are listened too as well.

We can't go through life saying anything to anyone regardless of the ramification of those words. We must make a genuine effort to craft our words so that they work for good and not bad. Our words should make someone feel good. Remember our words are given freely, so we can all give a good word.

Our words must be clear and delivered with the right tone. This approach requires we stay on message with regard to both tone and language. In essence, we must be understood.

Communication is what the receiving person hears and understands; if not given clearly, it is meaningless. So clarity of message is imperative.

Your goal should be to stay on message for your audience. It's important you take into account your groups' understanding. This will determine your language and tone. Once those things are delivered clearly, you can spread your message effectively to others.

As you take those two variables into account, you realize most people don't act on something that is simply heard. Nine times out of ten they need to be inspired to take action. To that end, as the communicator you must prompt your team to listen. Here's your chance to do so with effective delivery.

The dictionary's meaning for the word hearing is *'perception by ear'*. It is one of our (5) senses by which noise is received. Someone says something and we hear it, without regard to action. Once we are in the presence of the sound, we hear the information.

You very seldom have a choice to hear or not to hear something. As long as you are within the range of the sound you will hear the information. This does not mean you understand it or will act on it. You can even make a motion that you hear what the speaker says; but, what does that mean? None of those things matter, if you are not called to action.

For a long time, I was comfortable with just dispensing information, without regard to people's actions. I was of the school that believed in putting information out there and having people choose what works for them. That approach is fine, if you live in your own little world. But we are a community of people who depend on each other daily. With that in mind, it is to everyone's benefit when we share information: that people listen and they act.

What is said as opposed to what is done is a fine line. To hear does not mean we remember or that we will act. So it is important that you move from being heard to being listened too.

First, let's ask ourselves these questions. When we hear something, does it move us? When we hear the words, does it call us to action? When we hear the voice, does it inspire? For those things to happen the audience must listen.

To listen requires one to be quiet, pay attention, acknowledge understanding, display eye contact and give feedback. If feedback is needed, the active listener will participate in the process. They understand and they have a vested interest in what is being said.

The listener must believe there is something he/she can gain from the information. They are in the room so they can hear the information; and they listen because they believe it is useful.
To become the person others listen to; require your words be good, beneficial and serve as a

call to action. Take for instance the quarterback of a football team, why does his teammates rally behind him? Why does he bring the team together prior to delivering the ball?

The quarterback brings his team together, motions the next play and collectively; the team puts his words to action. He prompts his wide receiver, running back and other skilled-players to action. This pushes the rest of the team to respond in their supportive role. If the team does not listened, the play the quarterback called will not happen.

Now that we have established the importance of people listening, we must make sure they do that. No one wins if you speak and there is no action. A good leader prompts the team to action.

In my role as facilitator for many training sessions it is imperative that I set the right tone and deliver a message that strikes a chord. This information must have a common purpose. I have to make sure my audience is tuned into the message. I speak at a pitch that is loud enough to be heard yet clear enough to be understood.

Eye contact is important; this insures the team is in tuned with me as I am with them. Prior to speaking, I review the area for possible detractors to the message. I begin with positive remarks to gain the groups 'attention and assurance.

Knowing the power of the word, and its ability to move people to action, I try to deliver a message that the team can use quickly. This approach will build your reputation as one who can move people to action. This will only happen when the group listens.

As we move more and more people to action, we become more effective. The measurement of your communication will not be based only on what you say, but how you say it, and how it is received. People must understand you, they must feel a need to act and feel determined to spread your message to others. This is effective communication. People will hear, but when they listen, they are more likely to act on your words.

3) Is my advice sort after

Now that you are an effective communicator, what will you do with it? Now that you can move people to action, what role will you play in their lives? How will you use this to further your message?

Former President Ronald Reagan once said, *"We all win when one takes the credit."* A man who was once the leader of the free world was willing to sacrifice acknowledgement for victory. That says alot. When I think of those words, I think of things greater than myself.

Once you have a goal that requires more than your participation, you have to get others involved. To do so, you must strike a chord with them. You must believe in what you do and your ability to get it done. You must display a confidence in the project, and a strong desire to see it through.

Your objective is to get their buy in. They must see their role in your plan. They must believe the information you give will be helpful and beneficial to them. Once they recognize your helpful information, they will seek your advice and your counsel.

When you give advice you inform and notify others. You should be clear and precise; after all, by now you have mastered the art of communication. The advice you give should streamline the process.

You have now become the person who helps others find their way. To retain this role you must build a coalition of people who respond positively to your message. They may not agree with everything you say, but they understand, they respond to your message and can follow through on the mission.

Many times in giving advice, the closest people to you may differ with your objective. At times they may even put up a resistance; no need to be surprised. Their resistance becomes your challenge. And by facing this obstacle head on you become stronger and better.

This obstacle is a minor technicality or a small issue. You can overcome it by finding your leadership value, building other relationships and forging a larger network.

As you work on your network, begin with your childhood. Did your parents spend hours teaching you how to eat or walk or any of the basic things? Was it necessary for you to be shown the advantages of eating or walking? No.

You simply saw others doing it and immediately you recognized the benefit of it, and followed suit. You began practicing and imitating their behavior, because you saw the advantages for you. Your parents did not have to persuade you. You decided it was time.

A large part of giving advice is: knowing when the person is ready to receive it. If you want others to take your advice you must believe in the message and demonstrate its effectiveness. This is one way for others to seek you out. You should demonstrate your knowledge in an area where individuals have a need for your inspiration and they will find you.

They will come because they have that longing for themselves and they are searching for the answer to the same question. You have shown your knowledge in the area, and they come to you for advisement.

As your network grows, your advice to them should be relevant and essential. It should not be long or difficult, but effective and efficient. Individuals want what works, and they want it now.

The advice columnist, "Dear Abby" is world renowned and known for her common sense and useful perspective. She is in the business of advice, she found her niche. The same can be said for Ann Landers, who has been dispensing advice for over 4 decades. Ms. Landers has become so effective at her task that ninety million readers worldwide seek and follow her counsel daily.

Your group may not be as large as those ladies' but they are no less significant. You want to provide something that matters; something that forges relationships. Since your ultimate goal is similar to theirs, let us break down what they do.

Both "Dear Abby" and Ann Landers do not claim to be experts in every subject. In fact their claim to fame leans more towards the practicality of the issue. They have at their disposal a wide array of information and people. They are not afraid to refer their readers to sources other than themselves for more details. Ann Landers, in particular, is proud of her sagacity, wit and abundant energy. Her team includes her staff, her family, and well-connected friends.

They understand the issues their readership face, and the publics' desire for quick solutions. From that concept they built their market. Their claim to fame is not just the answer but the common sense approach to getting it.

Those ladies assembled a network to support what they do. Their plan was simple; make it clear and easy to understand. With those things in place, the readers return time and time again for their counsel.

So as you give advice, make sure it helps; and it makes people feel good. Keep it short, keep it clear and deliver it well. Stick to what you know and your followers will continue to seek your guidance.

4) Is my advice used

As we gain more clarity of who we are, we recognize the need to build relationships and coalitions. We have to build a team of people who trust us and depend on us. They look to us for answers. They seek our guidance.

They come to us because we have displayed a clear understanding of what we do. We have proven the information we have is clear and necessary for others. In essence, we now have information others can use. So how do we get the information to them?

As an outsider looking in, it is important to identify what a particular group needs, and bring that information to them. First, we should make sure accessing the information is easy, because our job is to simplify not complicate.

All of us from time to time use experts for our gain. We seek out individuals who demonstrate mastery in their field. We seek their knowledge because we believe their answer will be right. No one seeks out someone who does not have the answer.

People look for advice from others to gain something. With that in mind, we must position ourselves to be the one to give the right information in the area of our expertise.

We know now how to give advice so now we must focus on what we do well and how people will use it.

The traveling salesperson takes his/her product on the road. They do this after they have identified where the need is. As new communities are built, furniture sales increases, they are in bigger demand. At times, salespeople will bring these items door to door making it easy for their potential customer to say yes.

The salesperson has a product and has identified the client for it. This is not a new concept; in fact, it is a simple concept. People will use what they need, and they will pay for a service. This is the ultimate value, merging deed with need.

Whatever you provide or do well, deliver it first to people who will need it and they will use it. This may require you to provide the service initially for free, so you can build a client base. The same client base may later provide testimony of your service or product. They could become the team who will recommend you.

They could speak to your integrity and passion. Their testimony will demonstrate your ability to move others to action. This team may be able to show others your inspiration, your passion, your work.

As you go forth with this team, you become more confident. Your action will be confirmed as people accept your product. You will speak on that subject with more authority while others speak of your good behavior and integrity. To insure that you maintain that mastery, stay abreast of all the trends in the field. To do that, your learning has to be continuous.

As you give advice and it is received, still continue to seek more information on the subject matter to broaden your knowledge base, your scope and your network. People will continue to use what you provide, so long as it works. Remember, the owner of the team will stay with the head coach as long as he/she wins.

Take for instance a baseball franchise; as long as the manager wins, his job is secured. The more he wins the better he can negotiate in his favor. As he wins more, he can help others to realize their potential. Hence the players on the team can now testify to the manager's ability. The manager can write his own ticket, because his skills will be sort after, he will be in demand.

The team must buy into what you are doing or plan to do. They must see their role in it and be willing to participate. It's always good when you can deliver a message that your team can put into action quickly; this sets the stage for big things.

Also beneficial is for people to see measurable advancements under your supervision. While you build this team you will run into several people. Many will want to be a part of your plan or goal; while others may not; you have to determine who will be on board and who will not. They may wish you well, or they may not. Some may even compete head on with you; don't let hurt feelings deter you; since such feelings can't help you win.

It's important that you don't wear your emotions on your sleeves. As much as transparency is a good thing, a confident outlook is better.

Seek a confidant, someone who will help you stay on track and encourage you to advance your cause. Remember your goal is to share your information, and make sure it is used to expand your plan. The more people you have in support of your network the stronger your team will be.

Build your team with your confidence of the product or information, and provide it to those who can use it. Don't store away your product; it is a violation of the *"Law of Use"*. You want to share it and have others benefit from it. Before you know it, the message will be out that you are a master of a particular craft.

Always keep in mind, advice must build someone's confidence – it must make them feel better about themselves. As you build others up, you become stronger.

Chapter 2 Recap ~ HOW DO PEOPLE SEE ME?

- Making people happy is priority one. When people feel good around you they will want to be in your presence.

- Your message must be clear and concise. Create the right atmosphere to engage people as you build your team.

- When people come around, you should bolster your message to maintain the team while developing segregates to support your goal.

- Your confidence must be based on your winning approach; this will encourage your team to use your advice; hence seeing you as the master of that craft.

III

How do I see myself

"All I need in life is ignorance and confidence; then success is sure."
Mark Twain (1835 — 1910), Letter to Mrs. Foote
Dec. 2, 1887

1) Am I happy

Now that we know our belief system will lead us to our passion. Once discovered, we should pursue it. Our passion will allow us to give advice to others that will grow our network. There is a process to this; first, start by being content as you develop your passion and grow your network.

Accept challenges and dissent, but don't let others define your fulfillment. When you continue to reach for your passion, happiness will be the outcome. And once you are happy, your goal will be attained.

Acknowledge who you are each day, affirm your roll and start anew. After all, you are responsible for your own happiness. The task at hand is to know when you are happy, and how to secure that happiness daily.

Most people will agree happiness is what they want; but do they know how to achieve it? When it's in their midst, what does it feel like? Are they able to bottle this happiness and pour it out like an expensive wine? The question of the day is, are we happy?

First of all we must know how to be happy. Happiness flows from inside. When we are content with where we are and where we'll be tomorrow; that is happiness.

Happiness can't be measured in things you buy; rather, it is based on a feeling. Those things that make you smile and say "aha", contribute to your happiness. It's that inspirational feeling, separate from outside challenges, and consistent with your ultimate goal.

The good thing about this inward feeling is: you can call upon it at any time. It can be a memory of a beautiful spring day, as you look out the window. It can be an email or a phone call that re-affirms who you are and who you can be.

Many people now are looking for a reason to be happy. They see gloom and doom and wonder when or if they can pursue their passion. It can be difficult, but as challenges come, prepare to rise above the obstacles.

I remember the first time I lost a job; it was a strange feeling. I was struck with worry and grief. Wondering how will I pay my bills? Isn't it strange how we think? Before I could think of me, my mind drifted towards the bill collector. So I was on a mission to secure another job. That was all I knew.

I never considered my well-being, my true identity or my happiness; my only focus was the next job. I secured the next job 3 weeks later, only to be downsized again nine months after. What does that say about me? Was I ready, did I jump in too fast? Whatever it was, clearly I was not happy. Surely I wasn't passionate about the opportunity. But thankfully, the second layoff allowed me to think about what I really wanted and what would challenge me to excellence. It was then that I decided to pursue my life's work.

I began writing resumes for friends and family, while doing job coaching with colleagues, and building my network. The website, business brochures, testimonials, the slide presentation, the mission and values of the company would come later. Within those six months of my second lay-off I saw a business develop, and a passion ignited.

But just as easily as you can find that spark you can lose it. I know that feeling well; you see, I fell into the web of the dream deferred. As soon as I got the call to another job, I put my dream on hold to help someone else attain their goals. I allowed the new job to delay my passion.

I dedicated myself again to another person's vision. Adding to this dysfunction, the job's mission and values were not aligned with my own. I experienced no joy in the peaks and no sorrow in the valley. I simply reported daily like a soldier. And worst of all, my compensation package did not come close to my expectation or my performance.

I was busy at it again working at a high level with unmatched compensation and a goal that had no relevance to me.

So what do we do when we find ourselves in that predicament? How do we bridge the gap? As hard as it may be, we must carry on. We must continue to perform with our eyes glued to the light at the end of the tunnel. We must roll up our sleeves and do what's needed today until we can get back on the road towards our goal. From time to time, we must call upon those joyous feeling, and re-direct our energies to what's needed for our happiness.

In the midst of both good and bad we must maintain our happiness. Keep in mind the two things that make us happy: our life's work and love. It's good to wrap yourself up in both.

2) Am I satisfied with being heard or do I need to be listened to

So you want to be happy. You want to experience that passionate feeling that motivates you to do more and be more. How do you do that? Are you satisfied with where you are? Is it enough? If you could change something in your life what would it be?

There are so many questions, and so little time. The truth is you have more time than you think. We all have enough time to do what we need to do. We just have to prioritize what we do and stay on course. I know, it's easier said than done.

We have already talked about how important it is to build that support team. We also know a good support team, built on mutual trust, will benefit us. So we press on and forge relationships with like-minded people. Every leader needs a sidekick, to support his/her agenda. Hence the importance of sharing information, giving advice and providing what people want and what they can use.

For a long time I thought it was disruptive to continuously challenge authority and be the voice of dissent. I looked at those people who did that as being difficult; when in fact, the basis to success is a good challenge. Dissent and criticism allows for mistakes to be corrected.

The same way you build a government, a company or a team: you need varying views to correct mistakes prior to launch. As you surround yourself with multiple views, you recognize the role of each member. To corral this group and assert yourself as leader you must deliver a clear message that allows for varying views. You must be passionate about your vision because you will have to defend it.

For a long time, I enjoyed gathering information and putting things out there. I also took pleasure in doing what was expected without getting full credit; I simple completed tasks. Many times I proceeded and completed each task, but is that the role of a leader?

I remember telling friends, I could just as easily work for my best friend or my worst enemy. I never followed the view of *"when the cats away the mouse will play"*. Completion was always my satisfaction. But is that the best performance of a leader?

I continued showing up to meetings, providing no dissent or opposing view. I would provide information as requested which guaranteed my place, for a while. In addition, I would deliver more than what was required and watch others take the credit for my work. When would I learn?

Simply providing what is asked will not be enough. In corporate America, as you complete each task, you'll be given another. This is the story of many people who have strived for individual excellence. If that is your goal, then being heard is enough.

Individual excellence allows you to be effective and task driven. This attribute is usually found in those without passion. They lack the motivation to fight for the view they believe in. They are simply operating like drones. They simply check off agenda items daily. If you are in this group then being heard is enough.

My most recent jobs have placed me in that category. I didn't challenge nor did I show dissent. I allowed others to paint me with a broad stroke and even speak for me. Were they always on my side... well I'll let you figure that out.

Just being heard does not separate you from the crowd. It simply puts you on the sideline of the team, the person who goes along and gets along. The problem with that scenario is, if you are not bringing anything different, your views may not be used at all. Your thoughts will be added to the big list that supports the mission.

The problem with this role is: you may not emerge as an expert in any area. The value of your contribution will diminish as time goes by and you will eventually be left out. Is that where you want to be, an outsider looking in. Or do you want to play an active role?

If you want to be active in this arena, then you have to fight for what you believe is right. If you are motivated and task driven: you have to show your tenacity and inspire others to listen to you. You must deliver a message that strikes a chord and brings others along.

The days of being an individual achiever is good; now you have to move up another level. As others listen to you, your team will increase and your role will grow. There will always be a place for the person who has several achievers singing their praises. It is true when they say good managers create other managers.

To insure your longevity, you must have staying power. You should continuously improve on what you do best, and perfect it. Show your excitement about what you are doing now, develop your issue, visualize your future and create your plan. If you are not excited; your team will know and they won't follow.

Trust your team to be your biggest cheerleader, and they will sing your praises. You have to make your mark, and the best way is when others listen to you.

You have not arrived at your goal until others listen to you. When others understand your message and they believe in your vision they will commit. When they have tested your approach, when they see you are truly vested and proud of your contribution they will support you.

This requires a level of confidence, but not too much. You don't want to alienate other achievers from joining your team. Just like the gallop polls have a margin of error you must allow for your lack of perfection. You will be elevated when your tent grows.

The only time you can be truly satisfied is when you are listened to.

This will drive you to get better. So when you have an opposing view, display your dissent, it allows you to be heard. When you do so with clarity and assurance it will inspire others to listen.

3) Am I a mentor, if so, do I enjoy it

Oliver Wendell Holmes said it best, *"...that what is given or granted can be taken away, that what is begged can be refused; but that what is earned is kept, ...that what you do for yourselves and for your children can never be taken away."*

The need to build solid relationships and have a network of dependable people is very important. It's just as necessary to identify your passion, and belief in yourself. When you couple that with a network of believers, who are not afraid to challenge you on your idea, you will remain motivated.

Those two things will provide a delicate balance that a good leader uses to succeed. Keep in mind the challenger also believes in the product and shares in your ultimate desire.

Once your team is built, you must keep the team on track. It's not enough to simply have listeners you must put those individuals to work. Allow them to help you shape your vision.

As you build a strong team, identify the ones who can best relay the message and then delegate responsibility. It is important that you do this to prevent overexposure of one person. Having multiply voices saying the same thing helps the leader, the mission and ultimately the organization.

It is important to have several voices, with the same message, this re-enforces your goal. It allows others to see the potential success of the project, and it serves as a support for the overall effort. So now to secure this loyalty, you must help others to be their best.

Don't look at team building as a burden; keep in mind 'high fives' are not done in isolation. You must be driven by this task; with the understanding when you give of yourself and bring others along, you feel better. Now is the time to be a mentor.

As a mentor, deliver a clear message: this quails confusion and builds confidence. You must support and encourage your group and recognize the good in your surroundings and connect with it.

There will always be someone to help those who ask. Your role as a mentor is to connect the two. As team leader your job will require you to bring together your deeds with clients' needs. Have your supporting cast show you who they are, and then you must put your cast in their right roll.

As the mentor for much of your network, make a point of listening to them. Continue to dialog your rhetoric, with eloquence, clarity and inspiration.

As you listen and provide feedback, understand your response must build up not destroy. Show them how to disregard bad advice. Teach them how to take on a victor's attitude; it will help shape them now and for the future.

Use your leadership to challenge them. Show them how to work their way out of victimization. Present them with the best way to guide their challenges toward their better angels.

It is true what they say; when you get too old to do, you teach. So teach them to balance irrational despair with hopeful optimism.

As for me, I have many mentors and treasure each one. I know the role they have played and continue to play in my development.

My mother being my first mentor; has played the role of conscience. She is the constant reminder of my upbringing. She points me in the right direction and assures my safe arrival. She has played the biggest roll in the navigation of my life. As I think of her I realize I am where I am today primarily because of her.

Being a mentor is an awesome feeling. It allows you to see your light shine in someone else. So embrace mentorship, it not only inspires a pupil but it gives the teacher a charge.

Remember as a mentor you have to encourage and enable others to succeed; this allows you to be even more successful. Appreciate the value in teaching and you will create more value each day. Your ultimate goal is to continuously repair, restore and renew.

As a mentor, you can't disappear in the background; you must remain in the forefront and lead. One of the joys of leading is to see the best of you in others. What better way to achieve this joy but to help mold and lead. Keep in mind, being a mentor is great.

4) Do I follow-up

As we teach and mentor others, we get an overwhelming feeling of pride. It is rewarding to watch someone blossom under your watch. As a former elementary school teacher, I was prideful when my students got the answer. I felt accomplished when they recognized how to solve the problem.

The ultimate joy of helping someone is when they get it. They understand the mission, and can be called upon to help deliver the goal. You start your network with like-minded people, who share your values and vision. Be prepared for disagreements knowing the team is aware of expectations.

To insure goals are met, you must follow-up. This is where many drop the ball. They forget the biggest part of the network. It's not enough to listen and share information. It's not enough to simply provide good feedback. You must constantly check on your team to make sure everyone is participating.

You can't just serve: you must inspire, you must challenge and insist on commitment. You must call on your team, make sure they are securing the right information and managing the data correctly. Keep them focused on what is needed.

When you follow-up, you secure your group. You motivate them. You encourage them and they become better. This encouragement must be continuous, because everyone won't fall in line with one speech. You can't expect to grow your network if you just disseminate information. The commitment to the goal requires more.

I remember joining a multi-level marketing company, and their team building process works in the same way. Their growth and success depend on a strong network. They are nothing without their family, friends and extension of people who fall under their line.

It starts when you join the network. From that moment you are treated special. The person who invited you is now a part of your up-line. That person's job is to nurture and protect you. They have to share their knowledge of the business with you. So it is imperative that they have a clear message with answers to your questions. They must help you build your network, since it will fall under their umbrella. They will be rewarded for the team they build and the team they help you attain. This requires a lot of follow-up; and will benefit the leader, the new member and overall team.

A good way to start is to use competencies to make connections. With that you hold your team accountable. You have to listen to their views, share your experiences, point them in the right direction and ultimately grow your network. This group is now an advocate and will be an effective voice for the mission. You must make sure they believe in the goal, support it and will defend it. Your job is to continuously follow-up to build future leaders, by motivating the group and igniting new visions.

The last thing you want to do is: give all the information away and not follow-up. You can't take for granted everyone will know what to do next, nor will they be inspired to go to the next level without further direction. Don't view this role of following up as a task, but as a tree reaching out to secure the branches.

The concept of following-up is a major component towards ultimate success. Many times we fail because we did not follow-up. We fail to encourage the same team that will help us get to the next level. We fail to inspire that team and they fall apart. When the team falls apart we lose. But when we follow-up we secure one of the biggest sections of our journey.

By fortifying your team, you no longer stick out, but your mission and vision will stand out. You can't get tired at this stage. You must be courageous; knowing this behavior is smart and reassuring.

So be steadfast with your relation and network building. Create a venue of individuals aligned with similar goals and plans for achievement. You can't rest until this part of your work is done, it is not enough to do, you must also teach. The essence of following up will insure your goal, your vision and your passion are attained.

Chapter 3 Recap ~ How do I see myself?

- ❑ The importance of recognizing what makes you happy. Tapping into that energy when you need to.

- ❑ Identifying the difference between being heard as opposed to being listened to. Do what you must to capture the groups' attention.

- ❑ The importance of being a mentor and relishing the role. Knowing the mentorship roll will allow you to attain a great sense of pride and accomplishment.

- ❑ The need to follow-up to secure and maintain the group and eventually allow for expansion.

IV

Dream, Plan, Execute and Achieve

"I will prepare and someday my chance will come."
Abraham Lincoln (1809 — 1865)

1) Dream big, and in color

Knowing who you are, how people see you and most important how you see yourself, will allow you to dream big and in color. So many times we minimize our goals and dreams for one reason or another. We take on the safe role of what has worked in the past and stick to those areas of comfort.

When that happens, idealism has left our world and we become too practical. We build a wall around ourselves and invite fear to reside in the open spaces. After building the wall, we become afraid to climb around it because we are unsure of what's there. Adding to that, many of us neglect to build a team, so we have no one to help us see beyond the wall. With this lack of planning and lack of team building we have no one to take the vision on the road. We become cynical, we may drift from job to job, or worst, we may stay with one company and never pursue our dream; never take a chance.

Thankfully, we are not in those groups. We know who we are. We have built our team; they see us in a positive light and stand ready to deliver our message. We gain strength from the links we have built, we see ourselves as mentors, motivators and bearers of the dream. Most of all, we are no longer afraid.

We adhere to the law of non-resistance, where we face down the obstacle. We see each obstacle as a non-starter which allows us to clear it out of our path to success. Based on what we have done, our dream has become our goal. Now we must plan to make it big and fill it with bright colors.

We realize building walls will limit our dreams and our goals. Now that we see ourselves in leadership we should take action.

Part of our goal is our mission, which should be to achieve our potential within a necessary timeframe. To do so we must first look to our past. See what others have done with similar skills and behavioral traits. Know that their success can be our success. When we put those things together we project a better future for ourselves, and our team.

Ideally, we should pursue our dreams like Dorothy did in "The Wizard of Oz"; where she used the "Yellow Brick Road" as her road map home. Like Dorothy's team, we have to embrace the Heart of the Tin Man, the Courage of the Lion and the Brain of the Scarecrow, while keeping our eyes on the Emerald City. In our dreams, our goal is the Emerald City, and our path is to conquer those things that stand in our way.

So as you dream that colorful dream, don't limit your imagination. See yourself achieving the goal with each step. It's not that far away and it is not out of the box for you; rather, it is meant for you. It is a part of your purpose; allow it to become a part of your life.

Decide what's needed to make your dream a reality. Determine who you will need to advance your vision. Continue to demonstrate how the dream will unfold, and how each member of your team will benefit. The same way your dream captured your imagination; it should inspire others to join and help. Although it's your dream, you will need others to help make it real.

Start with the group who listens to you, the group you mentor. You built that team for a reason, they are your network; lean on them. They will give you the perspective you need to organize the dream. Even though it is your dream, you can't do it alone.

We have to dream big and in color. Don't be afraid of sharing the dream, the larger the team the greater the chance for success.

Think of your success like the great baseball movie, "Fields of Dreams". Where the lead character believed if you build it, they will come.

It is in that spirit; you must build your field of dreams and allow great things to come.

So as you see yourself in your special place, the dream becomes more and more real. You will spend less time dreaming about the future, and more time planning for it. Taking you big dreams to the planning stage is all based on what you do today.

2) What is my motivational level

Let's re-visit who we are? Let's make sure we know what we believe. Also, our purpose is well defined and our passion is alive. Now let's get motivated to carry it out.

We know we need a solid team, that is fired up and ready to go. Our team has bought into our passion. They listen to us, they seek us out and they use what we say. We provide the right mix of structure and mentorship for them.

Keeping the team together requires motivation. This reminds me of an unemployed man I met who was filled with hope. He believed his current state was a fleeting moment and he would make it through this stage of his life. Even though he was unemployed he continued his goodwill donations.

His outlook on life was remarkable. After all, it would be easy for him to get discouraged, but he was not. On the contrary, he talked of his plan if things got unbearable. The plan included taking in a roommate, if he could not meet his obligations. This remarkable guy believed he would get pass this stage of his life. He recognized this was a bump in the road; and his outlook for the future was still bright.

All this from a man who may not have been the most educated; but he was hopeful. His story is one of sincerity and realism. His sheer determination allowed him to develop a strategy to maintain his desire. He knew exactly what he had to do. So when he encountered obstacles, instead of allowing them to derail his plans, he remained motivated while celebrating victories regardless of size, through his journey.

His unemployment status was a challenge; and he used it as a time to develop an alternative path to achieving his goal. So how do we remain as motivated as he seemed to be?

Begin by inspiring others, do so knowing your dream is not that far away. Keep in mind your challenges are mere stumbling blocks and develop a strong mind to overcome them.

Many believe the world is made of two types of people. One who sees the glass half empty and the other who sees the same glass half full; neither is wrong...the question is; which one are you?

The motivated person sees the half full glass. They continue to build on what they have started. They see the light at the end of the tunnel.

If indeed the world is made of just two types of people, then you have to determine which one matches your character best.

There is a method to the 'half empty glass person'. You see that person knows when to let go of a particular practice. When things will no longer change in their favor, they let it go and begin something else.

Still our world is a little more complex, we aren't just two types, it's not always black or white; but there are shades of gray. That's where the third person is. The person who sits in the middle, with no dominant force. They continue to develop creatively. They allow things to unfold, and make adjustments where needed.

They are motivated enough to try and have the courage to fail. They are not afraid of fighting for what they believe and they are ready to leave if circumstances dictate such behavior.

The more motivated you are the more likely you will utilize both tactical and strategic ways to attain your goal. The tactical approach requires the use of the available means to reach the goal. As the leader you will measure individuals' contributions. Tactically, you'll develop key measures and verify what each team member is doing. This process takes you from one task to the next.

On the other hand, the strategic thinker prompts the team to carefully create "best practice" for achieving the goal. The strategist plan is always in development.

Both tactically and strategically continue to motivate while maintaining practicality. This is not a fearful approach; rather it is a focused one.

From time to time, your role may shift from team leader to cheerleader. Primarily, your job is to remind the team of the goal: what's needed and what has already been achieved. Since winning is a habit, remind them of what they have done right and where they have already won.

It is important to note when you feel blocked in. When you need to renew and make improvements; so the team can thrive. Keep in mind your assignment, and never lose track of your success and achievements. That winning spirit will motivate you to do more and be more.

3) What is the time frame from dream to plan

As you develop your plan, it has to be about your interests and your goals. When you make it about you, you are in the driver's seat and in control of your destiny. First take note of your strength and use it effectively. As you continue to do more and be more, work on your organization, help them become more efficient. In essence, within the time frame of your dream to your plan, capitalize on several areas to seize your best opportunity to achieve your goal.

Good timing, superior perseverance and good intelligence will move your plan forward. Build your plan on the blocks of the past while putting things in place for the future. With lively passion, share your message. Use diversity to maximize your plan with clear communication.

As you spread your message use your intuition. Remember once you believe it, the goal can be attained. So all you have to do is plan and believe the plan will work.

Your plan should show your belief in the concept and your knowledge of the market you will serve. The last component is to bring the deed and need together. This part will require a high level of motivation. It is the main part so inaction is not an option.

Failure to plan will only prolong the delivery of your goal. Once you plan, you must act and you must lead.

Over twelve years ago, I got my first recruiting job, where I secured the best temporary employees for Fortune 500 Companies. In my supervisory role, I managed well over 100 temporary employees, and collaborated with 9 other recruiting firms.

After doing this for several months, I learned the process well and perfected the project. The recruiting firm I represented was voted superior. The President of the Corporation, who was my client at the time, offered me the full contract. He noted that it was my leadership that allowed the agency I represented to outperform the other staffing firms. He then suggested I create my own firm. It was an enormous opportunity with built in motivation.

My next step was to follow-up on his suggestion; but did I? Did I view his offer as a goal I could achieve? Did I jump right in and begin to plan?

Unfortunately I did not. I never seized the moment. I did not see myself in that role. So as time went by the offer went away and the plan was never created. I allowed time to pass without trying. Many times people talk about their "aha" moment; the moment when they seized the opportunity. Well that offer will forever be my "what if" moment.

I failed to build a model that could have worked. I neglected to construct a team that would sustain. At that point in my life my vision and action were not in sync. I failed to act. I didn't visualize myself in the role, so I could not plan; hence, I had nothing to follow.

If I knew then what I know now; I would have at least tried. I would have understood the importance of trying rather than avoiding the unforeseen challenges. I would have planned, concentrated and focused on some type of action.

I did not see the potential. I did not see my possible destination or my life in that direction. Basically, I did not take the bait, nor did I pursue options that would have allowed me to see clearly the path. I simply walked away.

Many times we fail to put a plan in place; so then we have no action or response. I should have seen the opportunity and capitalize on it. I should have understood the staffing firm's success was my success and it had earned me a seat at the table; where I should have cashed in. I already had a program in place, so all I needed was a team. That moment possibly was a missed opportunity indeed.

When given such an opportunity, it is important to define what success means to you. Then you should state your intention and how you will achieve it. You should leverage your strength to build a team that will achieve the goal.

Once you are ready to go, you must act in a timely manner; failure to do so will force you to react; hence taking away your position of strength.

You must recognize that no situation is hopeless. Whatever the circumstance, you can confront it; because the moment you start: you change it. Plan your foundation based on your goal, the occasion and your audience. Know what is expected, and be prepared to deliver.

Part of your planning will include connecting best minds with best practices to achieve the goal. You must allow the team to speak freely and affirm each member. The best way to do that is to assure them, their views will be taken into account.

Your plan should also be attainable and sustainable. One key requirement for accountability is to do your business in the light of day. Once you have assembled a great team, your group will generate a good product and be profitable.

The key to planning and taking action is to do so without fear of failure. If it didn't work the first time you can always try again. Act quickly but provide time for the plan to develop. You don't want to begin crafting your second initiative too soon; this may give off the impression that the initial plan did not work.

No plan is perfect, as the leader, your role is to motivate good people to do great things.

So today, go beyond the disappointments, begin to work toward the dream, and make the most of what you have been offered. Remember your goal is only a plan away.

4) Is the goal attainable

Creating the right plan, then perfecting the best plan, will require testimonials from various individuals to assure your teams' buy-in. The only way to know if the goal can be achieved is to execute the plan.

With a working plan as the model, begin to test it. With success as the ultimate goal, develop benchmarks to victory along the way. Have your analysis ready, so as soon as you realize your approach isn't working, adjust the plan. Stay on pace, maintain your motivation and note your progress daily.

While you are going through this trial by era process, be grateful for what you've learned, and use it to move ahead. It is imperative that you are self-assured and believe you will accomplish the desired result.

I remember when I started my resume business. I was excited. I developed the concept, wrote the plan, launched the website and created a slide presentation. Later I designed some flyers and brochures and adjusted my email auto signature to include both a link to my website and the business slogan. I pulled together almost 1,000 emails and sent out several email blasts. With all that, I still continued my regular 9-5 job.

I did all those things but neglected to do the last thing…follow-up. I did not put my efforts into what was needed to achieve my goal. I did not fully invest in me.

I did not spend enough nor did I seek investors. I did not show my belief in the plan and worthiness of the goal. Had I pursued it vigorously, who knows what would have happened; maybe the resume business would have really taken off. And if it didn't work: I would have learned from it and moved to "Plan B".

As we continue to test our plan, we must manage the project. Though plans change the ultimate goal remains the same…success.

As we achieve each goal we win, but it won't come easy. To win requires a sustained effort with persistence. We must stay the course and continue to do those things that have worked and let go of those ideas that have not aided our efforts.

Our choices must be based on the evidence we have and primarily the ones that worked. By doing this, we will establish *"best practice"*. All those past accomplishments will lead to present day successes. Most of all, you will find out what you're made of when you try.

Don't worry about failing; keep in mind some of the best businessmen failed several times before they got it right. Even one of our greatest Presidents: Thomas Jefferson said, *"...we would need dramatic change from time to time"*.

History tells us President Jefferson did not sit on the sidelines hoping for the best, he engaged in a plan to secure victory. He negotiated with France to buy the Louisiana Territory. And he commissioned Louis and Clark to pioneer the west. He played a big role in building our nation. He was a visionary who continued to plan.

So as we look at what he did and how he did it, we too must revamp our plan and engage various people. As the leader, we have to be willing to move people around and revamp the tools they need to succeed.

Since timing is everything we have to be ready to act and be able to measure our success continuously. Our results must be detailed and clear to minimize crisis situations. Though we shift from time to time, high expectations must be set and achievable. We have to maintain the team's attention to move ahead. Each team member should be briefed on changes to the plan. Once they remain motivated, they will enjoy what they are doing and believe the end result will be achieved. Knowing there is a benefit at the end for them, the effort will come more easily and with greater effectiveness.

The goal can only be attainable if you try. So give yourself the power to try right now. Test your plan for effectiveness. Make sure this is something you truly enjoy and you will master it. Don't over think it; your action will be based on the tasks needed to achieve the goal.

A lot of goal attainment starts with believing in yourself. This reminds me of one of my nephew's school stories. This story is a tribute to the belief he has in himself. To hear him tell it, he begins with the results of a standardized test. Before the teacher returned the papers she gave the class a little speech about the importance of the test and how good many of them did. She then proceeded to distribute the papers; it was at that time my nephew told his friends he was certain he got the highest score.

Bear in mind; my nephew's confidence is always high, at times, it can surpass his effort. Even when no one gives him a fighting chance he believes he can. He never doubts his abilities. Though his friends laughed at his audacity; none of them took the bet, because they know he is a winner. And remarkably to no surprise, he did score the highest mark.

This just goes to show, all goals are possible if we believe and most importantly if we try.

Chapter 4 Recap ~ Dream, Plan, Execute & Achieve

❏ Big colorful dreams speak to a vivid imagination. One filled with hope and desire

❏ Your motivational level will be as large as you want it. Once you know who's on your team, have them play to their strength.

❏ Timing is important. First decide what you have to do; then do it.

❏ The dream and the plan must be attainable to keep you and your team in the game. As you get closer to the prize, push a little harder. Remember goals are attainable if you believe and if you try.

V

The Good Life

"Of course there is no formula for success except perhaps an unconditional acceptance of life and what it brings."
Arthur Rubinstein (1886 – 1982)

1) How does someone live well

Earnest Hemingway spoke of the importance of understanding our world as opposed to just fighting for it. As much as we want success, we must understand what success is for us. How others see us is important to building our network but how we view ourselves is the real factor to our happiness.

Ultimately happiness has to be our goal, once that's established the actual goal will come easily. What makes us happy at various times is dependent on how we feel. Just like your personal style is fluid (always changing) so is your reasoning behind the happiness.

At times you may have to get suggestions to develop your plan. But by all means, make it simple and easy to understand.

Your true happiness should be filled with your passion and your comfort; the ultimate balancing act, and together they will lead to contentment. Remember as you strive for your goal, look at it as having everything to gain and nothing to lose. This allows you to remain focused and motivated with the understanding that your goal is attainable. This is your happiness so take responsibility for it.

The same way you build your network, you will build your happiness. Begin first by taking an interest in what you are doing now. Do it with a smile and greater things will come your way. Become an expert in what you are doing and show your expertise to others. If they require your service, provide it freely, this allows for additional practice; and later you will find a market willing to pay for your service.

A couple of years ago, I attended a women's conference and had an extended conversation with the keynote speaker. At the time I was working for a non-profit firm. The speaker and I talked briefly about the mission of the organization and how the mission would help me shape my passion. The speaker advised me to first figure out my zeal; then begin to compile as much information on the subject as I can. He suggested that I put things in perspective, do the research and become an expert on the subject. He went further to say, put other things aside to insure I make the time for my specialty. In essence, he wanted me to narrow my vision, to allow for mastery of the skill.

Basically, he advised me to master my skill, promote it, and then bring it to the people who will pay for the service. With this concept you can live your life on your terms and live it well.

Even when your plan is clear and transparent, you will encounter some ups and downs, don't let that stop you. Continue to build your network so when challenges arise you can lean on your team for encouragement.

Your happiness requires that you live life to the fullest, show interest in what you do and collect as many things about your vision as possible. Know that your team is on board, and they are committed to excellence.

As their leader, they will challenge you to do all you can; and make the right choices. They will motivate you, but you must make the ultimate decision and follow it through. Once you choose, it will raise your understanding and overall life.

Take time out each day to clear your mind and heart, so you can focus on your passion. As you do those things, wish others well, and surround yourself with like-minded individuals. Don't be afraid to stay in the background at times, this allows new leadership to stand-up. As you help others, they will support you.

Allow your network to see the positive action you take and how it improved other areas of your life. They will recognize your work was used to grow, build and accomplish great things. They will see your confidence, your release of doubt and your progress. They will see the effectiveness and happiness that surround you.

When you accomplish that, you can begin to enjoy the challenge of working with intensity. You will be most productive, most effective, and committed. The more you work the more you'll accomplish. And then from time to time, sit back and enjoy the fruits of your efforts. Be your own cheerleader and live in the present for the joy of it.

Keep in mind you are an individual, and what you do makes a difference. Your goal is to attain a life full of meaning, tranquility and sheer joy. Allow your best to flow and don't be afraid of falling in love with life again and again.

Recognize the unique quality in each situation, while focusing on bringing value to your life. As you create this value, remain calm. Understand your team, respect them and wish them well; as you do this, they will feel the power of your purpose.

As you navigate your way through this journey, discouragement may set in from time to time. You may drift away from your comfort zone. Don't go too far away; remember when this happens seek out advise from your mentor. As you do this: your mentor will likely become one of your biggest supporters. They will support you as you set the tone with a more effective plan.

To live a life full of wellness you must know who you are, what you like and stay ready to make adjustments. Never stop working at fulfillment, because as you do well you will live well. Remember you can't go wrong by getting better.

2) What is the cost for living well

You dream, you plan, you follow through on the plan and you achieve it. Also, you realize if the first plan did not work, make adjustments where needed to achieve success. Ultimately you want to win, you want to live well you want to be happy. The question is: At What Cost?

What are you willing to sacrifice to insure your happiness? What are you willing to do to secure fulfillment, inner peace and joy? Once you recognize what you want, you must make a decision to allow the vision to flow. After you put your team together for the purpose of securing the goal, be prepared to do things different, if needed.

Your vision may require you to leverage your power for the good of the team. Continuously show the group, with innovation and charisma, how they benefit by following your plan.

Many of us watch our co-workers rise within the ranks, and we wonder how they are moving so quickly. A few of them are working day and night and sacrificing everything they have for their jobs. Still many are learning the culture of the work place and are doing what it takes to move forward. They are working ethically, supporting their supervisor and allowing for mentorship to take place naturally.

The workplace like every other place operates with a "quid pro quo" (this for that) format. Those who understand that process; do and say the right things to insure their place for the future. Many of them simply ask the right questions at the right time.

Management then provides the right answers to their followers. They also listen intensively to issues that require their attention. In the final analysis, they provide support when it's needed knowing it will ultimately benefit them. The simple approach is to do little things, because they add up to big successes.

As you support others, you gain in strength. Although the vision is yours, you will need others to help you build it. You will need the team to lessen the cost. As you face tough choices, they will help you determine best practice. Your team has joined forces with you for the single objective...to win.

This group recognizes your knowledge and they are sold on your message. They are motivated by your purpose and passion and are continuously drawn in by your confidence and assurance. As a team leader and winner, your humble approach makes it clear that there is no room for arrogance. You must promote the concept of winning with no one taking individual credit. The ultimate cost will require you to try with an understanding that you may fail. This is the cost of your dream, your goal, and your vision. The ultimate sacrifice is the willingness to fail.

Before diving in, you should test the plan several times. You should speak with others in similar situations to insure best practice. You should analyze the risk to better manage the process. Your team will remain as focused as you, but keep in mind: This Is Your Vision.

Your role requires you to spread the central issue with your best perspective. As long as your team sees the big picture they will continue to invest and this will allow for a successful outcome.

The cost of living well will require preparation, determination and perseverance. You must have a fearless nature, and recognize the difference between stress and pressure. Remember you are pursuing something you love, though you may encounter challenges, those setbacks should not stress you out. Keep in mind the benefits that you strive for outweighs the initial cost.

3) Does the end justify the means

A football coach once said, *"...we play to win the game"*. I remember when I heard it for the first time; it jolted me to a new realization. No one plays to lose. No one prepares for a loss, or to have something done wrong. Each one of us plays to win.

This is where you work out the kinks, tweak the sections that may not flow, and fine-tune the package to assure the plan is a winner.

We've talked about doing what you believe in. Remaining passionate, keeping yourself motivated and building your network, while developing your dream. We know that success requires following-up and mentoring. We've dissected the dream for its visionary areas and its attainability. And realize it is within our reach.

Once we do those things and know it will make us happy; our lives will be more comfortable and serene. We recognize the cost, and come to the arena willingly to pay. So now the new questions are: Is this the best you can do? And are all the parts of the plan necessary?

As you travel down this road, with your plan in hand; you are ready to execute while making some concessions and compromises. Don't allow inaction and incompetence to prevail. Continue to be effective and efficient.

Review mistakes to insure they're not repeated. When those areas are identified, be prepared to seize the best opportunity to win the day. Begin early with a focus on the goal.

You have made the necessary investment in your team, and they are on board to the end. You've opened the field to allow the team to share ideas, so they can contribute to the overall success.

You have done those things, knowing what you want. Your justification will be based on how much you want to achieve the goal. You must continue to invest the time. When you give of yourself, you show the value of the goal you seek. Now as you review the plan and understand the cost, show your willingness to pay.

As the lively leader, your team will become more robust and ready to go. You've charmed them, yet served as their biggest critic when needed. You've cleared your mind and advised your team to downplay the obstacles; by reiterating there is much to do. This team, with constant motivation, will begin to see your vision as a reality.

As you progress, you begin to see the end product, and your dream will come alive, this will free you. Finally you can say, 'I've delayed this for too long'. I've spent too much time in the background, watching things happen. Not knowing if there was a place for me. Now you know there is; and you can see it.

You have every reason to justify your actions. You've been bent, but not broken. You see where others have invested in you so now you must invest in yourself. You see the end clearly; so disregard what you're going through and focus on what you're going to do. You know part of your investment will be time consuming, so as each day goes by, continue to believe in the endeavor, and give the full measure of devotion. In essence, stay the course

This is for you, it is your future; it is what will make you happy. As you stay on track become the immovable object, selfless, committed to the end. Continue to have faith in your future. This is your plan, it's your project; you are the heart and soul of it. So when the dust clears your vision will be what remains.

Your passion should be supreme; however you should allow for other teammates' view. You are constructive with your approach without being destructive in your dissent. So as others doubt your pursuit they won't affect your steady pace.

You speak as a visionary, and you know where everything is and your place in it. As you look around you, you see yourself winning.

You've tested this plan several times, and it has worked. Success is now yours for the taking.

You've answered the questions and your critics. You've kept your team together. The end is near and you feel good about what you've done, so enjoy your journey.

Take an active role in your life. Others may have helped you shape it, but you must build it. As you do those things, enjoy the process of fine-tuning those parts so your life reflects the best of you. Then and only then can you say the ends justified the means.

4) Did the journey make you smile

Lao-Tzu said, *"A journey of a thousand miles must begin with a single step."*

We have come full circle. From what makes you smile, to: are you smiling at journey's end? You have the knowledge, you have devoted the time, you have planned; basically, you have done the due diligence. What's next? That's the easy part; it's the smile. The smile comes when you see the fruits of your labor. It shows up as you pursue your profit. It comes alive while you are having fun.

When you enjoy what you are doing, your performance level increases and people are excited to be a part of your team. People see you as a winner while you help others win. As you are excited about what you are doing you become more effective and more efficient. People will find you engaging and compelling.

Though you are only responsible for yourself, you should welcome the opportunity to make a greater contribution to others. Your personal growth is your winning approach. Your ability to affirm, to leverage and be accountable; and by helping others you will shine.

Even at this stage, there are times when you can get blind sighted; and lose your way. What do you do then? During this journey, you must continue to craft your response to each event, to set the direction for your life. What keeps you smiling is when you choose the best option with the greatest value for you. You must be about doing good things, since it is better than just saying it.

At times the choice may offer an exit from the journey to explore other things for inspiration. So as you move through the process remain alert for new treasures, and stay motivated. You don't have to strive for more; rather, your mission should be to accept and celebrate what is.

Make sure you are meeting the expectations you set. Recognize the abundance that surrounds you, and you will achieve whatever you expect.

Your team is behind you and they are in place, so don't isolate yourself. If you choose to put up walls, they will isolate you from the great life that awaits you. Get rid of the fear of making a mistake; remember it takes a lifetime to become all that you are meant to be.

Your journey through this life of abundance is not far away. So keep smiling knowing the extra distance you take will be to your benefit. Your happiness will come not from the things you have but from the things you will do.

Your team will recognize their success is tied to your success. So as you continue to lead, do so with enjoyment. Make your environment even better and your team will treasure and value your opinions. They will see you for who you are…someone of value and merit. They will follow you and speak well of you. This is your team; you have brought them together; that alone is gratifying.

As you approach each day, be satisfied and confident. Make adjustments and adapt, build and modify so you can thrive. Use your energy towards more meaningful purpose. Keep in mind that you are fulfilling your hopes and dreams, so continue to inspire your team. Don't allow their value and your dream to drift apart. As you inspire, take time to celebrate and show gratitude.

Your goal is to be the soft and dedicated leader; it goes a long way towards building a solid and strong team. The journey towards success will be filled with many situations; good and bad, you will constantly have to choose. As you adjust, redirect and reaffirm, be mindful of your time. In those moments, demonstrate the *"Best You"* and you will live in a world where *"Life is Good"*.

When it's your passion you will smile and when it's your dream you will feel wonderfully alive. This life is yours, so experience the richness that it brings. Enjoy the opportunity to experience the good that comes your way.

You are about to take on a new venture, and it's what you want, so embrace your decisions. Approach it with a confidence and a fulfilling attitude.

As for me, when obstacles come my way I reflect on what Dick Gregory said at Marvin Gaye's funeral: *"Marvin Gaye's smile was like a good day in June."*

May your journey be filled with joy like good days in June.

Chapter 5 Recap ~ "The Good Life"

- ❏ Recognize how to live well, and do those things that will provide the life you want.

- ❏ Identify the cost of the good life and make sure you have the things in place to pay the required price.

- ❏ The means must be justifiable for you to truly enjoy the end.

- ❏ At the end, the journey should make you smile while you enjoy each moment.

10 - TIPS FOR A BETTER LIFE

1. Walk each day and smile; it's an anti-depressant.

2. Enjoy a daily dose of silence.

3. Make someone smile each day.

4. Don't waste time on gossip, on issues of the past, or things out of your control. Invest in positive energy.

5. Don't skip meals.

6. Don't take yourself too seriously.

7. Agree to disagree.

8. Make peace with your past.

9. Situations are always changing.

10. Stay in touch with your friends, they'll care for you when you are sick.

"Those who are attentive to a matter will prosper ...-- Proverbs 16:20